Major Competitive Reality Shows:
Dancing with the Stars

Robert Grayson

Mason Crest Publishers
Philadelphia

Mason Crest Publishers
370 Reed Road
Broomall, PA 19008
www.masoncrest.com

CPSIA Compliance Information: Batch #060110-MCRS. For further information, contact Mason Crest Publishers at 1-866-MCP-Book

First printing
1 3 5 7 9 8 6 4 2

Library of Congress Cataloging-in-Publication Data

Grayson, Robert, 1951-
   Major competitive reality shows: Dancing with the stars / Robert Grayson.
      p. cm. — (Major competitive reality shows)
   Includes bibliographical references and index.
   Includes webliography.
   ISBN 978-1-4222-1673-6 (hc)
   ISBN 978-1-4222-1936-2 (pb)
   1. Dancing with the stars (Television program)—Juvenile literature. I. Title.
   PN1992.77.D32G73 2010
   791.45'72—dc22
                              2010015970

791.4572
G

Contents

1

Fascinating Rhythm

For a television network, it was a daring, bold move—a reality show about ballroom dancing, but with a twist. Take celebrities and teach them how to dance—really dance. But would the concept work? Could a championship boxer learn to cha-cha, a famous soap opera star learn to rumba, a beautiful model learn to tango, a well-known boy band singer learn to samba in just a matter of days and then perform those dances on live television? And what about the financial risk? Would anyone out there in TV land care?

As it turned out, people certainly do! *Dancing with the Stars*, or as it is better known to its fans, *DWTS*, is currently one of the most popular shows on television. *Dancing with the Stars* attracts an average weekly audience of between 21 and 25 million viewers per show. With two live shows airing each week, that is a lot of eyes watching the dance floor. On every show, celebrities *vie* for votes from a panel of three judges and millions of viewers as they battle to become the season's *Dancing with the Stars* champion.

6 Dancing with the Stars

This reality dance show, which has two "seasons" a year, manages to combine many of the elements of great television in one package. *DWTS* offers good entertainment, solid competition, nail-biting suspense, an uncertain outcome, and meaningful viewer participation. In addition, the show is broadcast live before a studio audience in Hollywood and because it is so popular, almost anyone is likely to be in the rows of onlookers, fans, and well-wishers. Such celebrities as Queen Latifah, Paula Abdul, Henry Winkler, Ashley Tisdale, and LaToya Jackson have all been seen when cameras pan the seats. The studio audience for *DWTS* is the place to be—and to be seen.

NO SECOND CHANCES

Because it is live, the show gives off all the electricity of an opening-night performance every time it airs. There are no do-overs here, no second chances—anything can happen, and it often does. There are dynamic performances, slips, falls, and injuries, but the show must go on, even if nobody knows whether a celebrity will answer the call when the time comes to take to the dance floor. It is a stressful, energy-laden stage, and even the most seasoned athletes, actors, models, and singers seem to be sweating as their big moment on the unforgiving dance floor arrives.

One of those teaching the celebrities the ropes, professional dancer Tony Dovolani, told *TV Guide* magazine: "We're teaching these guys dances that take years to learn in four days. So, yes, the tension was high."

Fast Fact

Celebrities who are thinking about being on *DWTS* often visit the studio to watch a few shows before making the commitment. So when fans catch a glimpse of a star in the audience, rumors start flying about a prospective appearance on *Dancing with the Stars*.

Since the program first aired in 2005, viewers have seen singers, football players, actors, boxers, Olympic champions, a racecar driver, a rodeo champion, and a talk show host morph from ballroom duds to dazzling hoofers. The final show of each season, where the champion is crowned on live television after weeks of grueling dance routines, always sparks heated debate and great anticipation.

THE TALK OF HOLLYWOOD

During the weeks that each show airs, the celebrities on *Dancing with the Stars* are the talk of Hollywood. The lagging careers of some actors and entertainers who have appeared on the show have benefited from a jump-start thanks to the publicity. Ty Murray, the greatest rodeo champion of all time, saw exactly what impact the show had when he left the saddle for the dance floor during the show's eighth season. "For me to be able to do this is a fantastic opportunity," Murray told the *Kansas City Star.* "You don't realize how big something like this is until you're on a show that 25 million people watch."

Donny Osmond, a television star during the 1960s and 1970s, rekindled memories of his youthful stardom during Season 9 of *DWTS* when he used fancy footwork and the instincts of a

Celebrities who appear on *Dancing with the Stars* compete for the coveted Mirrorball Trophy.

8 Dancing with the Stars

After ten weeks of entertaining drama and dazzling performances, Shawn Johnson and her professional partner, Mark Ballas, were crowned champions of *Dancing with the Stars*, May 2009.

veteran entertainer to dance his way to the championship. At age 51, he was the oldest winner ever.

In Season 8, Olympic gold medal gymnast Shawn Johnson became the youngest to win the title at 17 years old. She drew on her athletic skills to narrowly beat out French actor Gilles Marini by just 1 percent of the votes cast by the viewing audience. It was the closest outcome ever. Marini, a relative unknown in the United States before appearing on the show, gained enough attention from the narrow defeat to earn a role on the ABC drama *Brothers & Sisters*.

During Season 6, which aired from March to May of 2008, Kristi Yamaguchi impressed audiences with her moves on the dance floor. An

Olympic ice skating champion in 1992, Yamaguchi showed that she was as comfortable in dancing shoes as she was on skates. She became the first woman to win the *Dancing with the Stars* championship since the show's first season in 2005. The judges said the ice skater was the program's most consistent celebrity dancer ever, and gave Yamaguchi high scores for her dance routines throughout the sixth season's 10-week run.

One of the *DWTS* judges, Carrie Ann Inaba, has explained that the show is popular because it is inspirational. During an appearance on *The Oprah Winfrey Show* in 2008, Inaba said, "I definitely think it's about watching people who we look up to and aspire to be like getting out there and trying something new and really going for it. They're way outside their comfort zone, learning something new."

Marketing Quickstep

The success of *DWTS* has made stars of many of the professional dancers who appear on the show. That has set the stage for a marketing bonanza. Among the product tie-ins are video games, mousepads, color photos from the show, calendars, and posters. The most popular items, though, are exercise DVDs. Many of the show's professional dancers can be seen in exercise videos bearing the show's brand. The videos include *Dancing with the Stars: Dance Off the Pounds, Dancing with the Stars: Dance Body Tone,* and *Dancing with the Stars: Cardio Dance.*

Set to popular music, the DVDs teach fans of *Dancing with the Stars* how to lose weight while they learn how to dance with tips from the professional dancers who appear on the show.

Dancing with the Stars has become legendary for how much weight celebrities have lost while learning how to dance on the weekly show and the fun they have doing it. Far more enjoyable than a standard exercise routine, ballroom dancing has become a weight-losing craze as well as a popular exercise alternative, thanks to *DWTS*.

2

Shall We Dance?

Television networks in the United States were hardly battling each other for the right to air *Dancing with the Stars* when a British producer first proposed the idea in late 2004. In fact, the concept was turned down three times by different networks before ABC decided to take a chance on the program in March 2005. ABC executives later said that they chose to air *Dancing with the Stars* because the show's concept was so unusual.

One thing that made *DWTS* stand out from other reality television shows at the time was that it was meant to be fun. On other popular programs, such as *Survivor* and *Fear Factor*, contestants lied and cheated in order to gain an advantage, or had to perform disgusting stunts. *Dancing with the Stars* was intended to be more light-hearted and positive. "It is a reality show without a mean bone in its body," *DWTS* host Tom Bergeron explained on *The Oprah Winfrey Show* in 2008. "There is no bug-eating or **backbiting** or anything like that."

ABC was not taking a risk on a show with a totally untested formula, however. *Dancing with the Stars* was based on a popular British television series about ballroom dancing called *Strictly Come Dancing*. That toe-tapping show, aired by the British Broadcasting Corporation (BBC), had debuted the previous year, on May 15, 2004.

A EUROPEAN SENSATION

Ballroom dancing is very popular in Europe and has had a television following in England since the late 1940s. Britain's first TV program about ballroom dancing was a hit series titled *Come Dancing*, which ran on the BBC for nearly fifty years, from 1949 through 1998. It was one of the longest-running television shows in the world. *Come Dancing* started out as a program to teach people how to dance, with professional dancers Syd Perkins and Edna Duffield giving viewers instruction on the finer points of **sashaying** around the dance floor. The format changed in 1953, when the show became a ballroom dance competition.

Six years after *Come Dancing* was canceled, the idea made a comeback as *Strictly Come Dancing*, with professional dancers teaching celebrities how to dance. In this reincarnation of the long-running dancing show, celebrities would be scored on their dance performances by both judges and the viewing audience. Those with the lowest weekly score would be eliminated from the show.

The idea made it to the United States as a proposal for a show called *Dancing with the Stars*. Shows from the United Kingdom had an established track record in the United States. The successful game shows *The Weakest Link* and *Who*

Fast Fact

BBC producers searching for ideas for the British fall TV schedule in 2003 decided to dust off the old concept of a ballroom dance show, but toss in some celebrities to spice it up. That led to the development of *Dancing with the Stars.*

Wants to Be a Millionaire both start-ed out in England. So did *Pop Idol*, a talent show that became the model for *American Idol*.

DWTS producers knew that one of the show's hidden strengths was that each of the celebrities cast on the program would attract his or her own fans to the program.

NOT AN EASY SELL

Yet a show spotlighting ballroom dancing just did not get anyone's heart racing in the United States, admits *Strictly Come Dancing* executive producer Richard Hopkins. Nevertheless, after seeing how consistently the show drew large British television audiences, Hopkins was convinced that the concept would catch on in America as well.

So undeterred by earlier rejections, Hopkins met with ABC executive vice president Andrea Wong. After admitting that he himself secretly took ballroom dancing lessons, Hopkins got Wong to agree to watch an entire episode of *Strictly Come Dancing* from beginning to end, together with her staff. The idea was for her to see whether the episode captured her interest. It did. Hopkins later said, "The spandex, tantrums, and tor-sos had them hooked. Against all expectations, we sold the show."

The excitement over selling the show was short-lived. A lot of work had to be done to get a celebrity-driven reality show on the air. The toughest part was finding six celebrities who would be willing to dance on the show. The celebrities would be asked to dance all the ballroom standards, such as the foxtrot, the samba, the jive, the rumba, the waltz, the *paso doble*, the cha-cha, the quickstep, and the freestyle. None of the dances were easy, especially for novices.

Hopkins found that, in the United States, it was hard to get stars to commit to a television show—and a reality show, at that—especially if they had lined up or were hoping to line up something better to do, like a movie. "Even if you catch them [stars] 'resting' between movies, most celebrities shun TV," Hopkins later explained. "Nearly all of them would rather die and go to Vegas than do a celebrity show." Nonetheless, Hopkins and his team set about filling the six celebrity spots for the first program.

PUTTING IT ALL TOGETHER

For Hopkins, landing former heavyweight boxing champion Evander Holyfield for the first show was a major achievement. Holyfield was a well-known celebrity, and Hopkins believed that the boxer would attract sports fans to the show. Once there, he hoped that model Rachel Hunter, soap opera star Kelly Monaco, and reality TV star Trista Rehn Sutter would help keep them there. Rounding out the six celebritiy positions were actor John O'Hurley of *Seinfeld* fame and former boy band singer Joey McIntyre, who had been a teen heartthrob with New

Tom Bergeron was an award-winning television personality when he was hired as co-host of *Dancing with the Stars*. Here, Tom speaks with Trista Rehn Sutter and her partner, Louis van Amstel, during the show's first season.

Celebrity contestants gather on the dance floor with their partners during the first episode of *Dancing with the Stars*, which aired June 1, 2005.

Kids on the Block in the early 1990s. Six professional dancers were hired to teach these celebrities all the moves they'd need for the show.

To make the show a success, the producers had to find personable hosts, knowledgeable judges, and a no-nonsense, knock 'em dead band. They got them all.

Tom Bergeron and Lisa Canning were hired to host the show. Bergeron had a good amount of experience in this role. He had hosted the television game show *Hollywood Squares* from 1998 to 2004, and in 2001 began hosting the popular program *America's Funniest Home Videos*. Bergeron would provide *Dancing with the Stars* with quick wit and good-natured banter. Canning, the co-host, was an actress and *Entertainment Tonight* reporter.

The panel of judges on *Dancing with the Stars* includes (left to right) Carrie Ann Inaba, Len Goodman, and Bruno Tonioli. All have worked as professional dancers and instructors.

In assembling the panel of judges, the *DWTS* producers decided to import two of *Strictly Come Dancing*'s judges, Len Goodman and Bruno Tonioli. Both were professional dancers. They would be teamed with an American dancer, Carrie Ann Inaba. During the first season, the three judges quickly became a pivotal, interesting, and even controversial element of the show. Goodman, Tonioli, and Inaba exchanged lively opinions about the celebrities' dancing performances. They even discussed how the professional dancers worked with their famous partners. When debate among the trio became a bit heated, Bergeron always managed to step in with a pithy, timely comment that **defused** any hostility. It became an entertaining mix that worked like a charm.

MUSICAL MAGIC

Everyone involved in the show knew that music would be a major part of *DWTS*'s success or failure. The music had to be current, catchy, and performed with extraordinary pizzazz. As *DWTS* judge Len Goodman told Variety.com, "Music is the essence of everything. Without good music you will never get good dancing."

To meet the challenge, Richard Hopkins selected Harold Wheeler, an award-winning composer and conductor, as the show's musical director. Wheeler not only had to please the show's producers and directors, but he also had to provide music that made the celebrities and their professional dance partners happy. In addition, the music had to entertain the live television audience. Simply put, the music was a critical part

A Dancing World

In 2006 and 2007, so many countries were telecasting versions of *Dancing with the Stars* that the show became the world's most popular program among all genres, according to *Television Business International* magazine. Versions of the show could be seen in Argentina, Australia, Austria, Belgium, Bosnia Herzegovina, Brazil, Bulgaria, Chile, China, Croatia, the Czech Republic, Denmark, Estonia, Finland, Germany, India, Israel, Italy, Japan, Latvia, the Netherlands, New Zealand, Norway, Poland, Romania, Russia, Slovakia, Slovenia, South Africa, Sweden, and Ukraine, plus, of course, the United States and England.

The show is known under various names in different countries. Loosely translated, the show's title is *Mad about Dancing* in Denmark, *Dancing Stars* in Austria and Bulgaria, *Let's Dance* in Germany, *Dances with Stars* in Finland, and *Dancing for You* in Romania.

Kym Johnson is the only professional dancer to win a championship in two countries. She has appeared on both the Australian and U.S. versions of the show, and was a member of the winning partnership in both countries.

Fast Fact

A studio audience of 550 people watch each *DWTS* show from seats in the studio ballroom. Though stars and members of each dancing celebrity's family are usually on hand, members of the public are also allowed to view the show in person.

of the show. Following *DWTS*'s first show Wheeler's musical scores were as much talked about as the dancing itself.

Before the show could come together, the role the viewing audience would play in *DWTS* had to be decided. Producers wanted the viewers to have a voice. So after each show, viewers could vote for the couple they thought had given the best performance that week. Those viewer votes would be combined with the judges' scores, and the couple with the lowest score would be eliminated on the next show.

TOUGH TIME CONSTRAINTS

Planning the very first show in the series, which was scheduled to air June 1, 2005, was *grueling*. The show ran only an hour, but figuring in time for commercial breaks left just 42 minutes of airtime—a tight squeeze for six dances, the judges' comments, and a show recap. The production staff timed each of the dances. They were *relentless* about keeping each segment within the allotted time. The whole first show was rigidly planned.

All the work put into the show paid off. When *Dancing with the Stars* aired, 13.5 million people tuned in to watch. This was the largest audience ever to view the debut of a summer reality TV show. The ratings went up from there. ABC executives knew they had a hit on their hands.

3

Encore!!!

In television, the best way to end a season is with a cliffhanger, and *Dancing with the Stars* had one after the first season, even though it was not planned. When *General Hospital* star Kelly Monaco narrowly defeated *Seinfeld*'s John O'Hurley on the July 6, 2005, finale of Season One, fans demanded a rematch. ABC was more than happy to comply. Sensing a ratings bonanza, the network scheduled a 90-minute, head-to-head dance-off between Monaco, O'Hurley, and their professional dance partners on September 20, 2005. The results would be announced on a special results show two days later. For this event, only the audience votes counted, and this time O'Hurley came out on top.

The biggest winner in this event was actually *Dancing with the Stars*. The program had proven to be so popular that ABC did not want to wait until the summer of 2006 to put on a second season. They wanted Season 2 of *DWTS* to air by January 2006. And it did.

BIGGER & BETTER

Dancing with the Stars, Season 2, debuted on January 5, 2006, with more celebrities, more episodes, more drama, and a bigger viewing audience

Kelly Monaco and her partner Alec Mazo (right) learn that she has won the title of Ballroom Dance Champion. In the first season *DWTS* finale, Monaco beat out John O'Hurley and his partner Charlotte Jorgensen (left) for the Mirrorball Trophy. In a rematch that aired two months later, fans of the show voted O'Hurley the better dancer.

than ever. There was a new co-host as well. Samantha Harris, a reporter for *E! News*, replaced Lisa Canning in that role. Ten celebrities took to the dance floor for the second season.

The first season only had six one-hour shows, plus the two dance-off episodes in September. For Season 2, ABC decided to air a 90-minute performance show on Monday nights, followed by an hour-long results show on Tuesday nights. The network was no longer afraid to run the show on back-to-back nights: *DWTS* had found its audience.

In Season 2, 15 episodes of the show would be broadcast over eight weeks. There was no results show following the season premiere in January, a week in which nobody was eliminated from the cast. ABC executives realized that *Dancing with the Stars* had managed to resurrect the family-style entertainment show and the results show gave the network a chance to present live, big-name entertaiment as the viewing audience excitedly waited to see who would stay and who would be eliminated from the show. The second season's results shows included live performances by Mary J. Blige, Barry Manilow, Burt Bacharach, the Pussycat Dolls, and Michael Bublé. Those performances often featured live dance numbers by top professional *hoofers* as well, some of whom were partnered with celebrities on the show.

The cast of celebrities included a number of well-known names; some of those stars turned into solid competitive dancers during the show. Former National Football League (NFL) star Jerry Rice, actress Lisa Rinna, professional wrestler Stacy Keibler, actor George Hamilton,

Samantha Harris (left) speaks with Jerry Rice and his partner, Anna Trebunskaya, moments after they received a score of 27 for their cha-cha in the Season 2 finals. Samantha became co-host of *DWTS* that season, and remained on the show until Season 10 in 2010.

and 98 Degrees band member Drew Lachey, among others, all tackled the dance floor. By the show's fourth week, producers calculated that each celebrity had already put in at least 100 hours of rehearsal time, and the competition was just starting to heat up. As the celebrity dancers got better and the judges' scores got closer, the viewers' votes grew more important.

'FISH OUT OF WATER' CONCEPT

Jerry Rice, who had become famous for catching passes as a record-setting wide receiver in the NFL, suddenly was snagging viewers for *DWTS* with his unexpectedly fancy footwork. Stacy Keibler showed that she could be graceful, making the switch from the wrestling ring to the dance floor. Viewers loved the "fish out of water" concept of the show. People who were very accomplished in one field were learning to do something new—and getting better at it as time went on.

The last weeks of Season 2 kept viewers on the edge of their seats. Drew Lachey and Stacy Keibler had dominated for most of the second season. Lachey was known for taking risks on the dance floor, while Keibler stood out for her technique. But in the last weeks, Jerry Rice and Lisa Rinna were coming on strong. Many disagreed when Rinna was eliminated from the competition on the next-to-last week of the show, but that only made the finals even more heated.

Fast Fact

Before one of the shows in Season 2, all the camera operators got locked out of the studio and could not convince the security staff to let them back in. With minutes to go before airtime and no camera operators in place, security officials realized that the folks outside the studio were telling the truth and let them back in just in time.

Drew Lachey's cowboy-themed freestyle dance with Cheryl Burke helped to propel them to the championship of Season 2.

In the finals Lachey and his partner, Cheryl Burke, put on a dazzling freestyle to the song "Save a Horse (Ride a Cowboy)," and *eked out* a victory. To the surprise of the viewers, Rice and his partner, Anna Trebunskaya, came in second, while Keibler and partner Tony Dovolani finished third. With his strong performance Rice showed that male athletes could compete successfully while still looking tough. Other men from the sports world soon followed in his footsteps. One was former NFL running back Emmitt Smith, who won the competition in Season 3.

With the success of Season 2, *DWTS* became a permanent part of ABC's weekly lineup. The show was considered a strong lead-in for new programs the network wanted to promote. ABC's plans called for *Dancing with the Stars* to air twice a year, with new seasons in the spring and the fall. To keep the show fresh, the producers would add new twists each season, like more celebrities, double eliminations, dance-offs to avoid elimination, and a kids' competition.

GREAT EXPOSURE

With Season 3, which began in September 2006, it became easier to get celebrities to come on the show and try ballroom dancing—even if the results were embarrassing. It was part of the fun, and the exposure added *incalculable* value to their careers. Even those eliminated from the show were invited to appear on programs like ABC's *Good Morning America* or the late-night show *Jimmy Kimmel Live.* Celebrities like Las Vegas headliner Wayne Newton, magician Penn Jillette, chef Rocco DiSpirito, Apple cofounder Steve Wozniak, politician Tom DeLay, and talk show host Jerry Springer have all danced on the show and been eliminated. All said they enjoyed the experience, and even returned to the show in later seasons when asked. Perhaps the only thing the now-willing celebrities did

And the Winner Is...

A lot of thought went into the scoring process for *Dancing with the Stars.* The show's producers were well aware that the celebrities on the show were not professional dancers; after all, that was the show's concept in the first place. In fact, the show avoids booking any celebrities who might have had any professional dance training, just to keep things fair.

The judges rate the celebrities on the elements of dance, from posture to dance steps, giving each performance a score from 1 to 10. The viewers, many of whom have no dance experience, can have their say by voting for the performances they like, regardless of whether they were technically superior. Viewers can even vote for celebrities just because they like them.

So *DWTS* scoring is not strictly a popularity contest, nor is it just a talent contest. Viewers can vote by phone calls or texts, or at ABC's Web site. A viewer can vote five times using each of the three methods. Voting goes on throughout the show and for half an hour after the show ends. When the voting period ends, the scores are tallied and combined with the judges' ranking. The couple with the lowest score each week is eliminated.

not realize was just how grueling and time-consuming it was to be on the show.

NFL Pro Bowl defensive end Jason Taylor likened his experience on the *DWTS* dance floor during Season 6 in 2008 with his battles on the pro football field. In an interview with NewYorkJets.com

just before the 2008 NFL season, Taylor said the competition on the gridiron and the dance floor is very similar:

> "You're still pushing yourself in your mind. [Learning to dance] is more about your mind than it is your body. You have to teach yourself to dance. You're athletic enough to move, but you have to get over the mental hurdles of figuring out what you're doing and pushing yourself through it."

Racecar driver Helio Castroneves already had two Indianapolis 500 titles under his belt before taking to the dance floor for Season 5 of *DWTS*. The hard-driving Brazilian was recommended for the show by the Season 4 winner, Olympic speed skater Apolo Anton Ohno. Castroneves, interviewed by RealityTVWorld.com, said Ohno told him how much fun it was to do the show: "And I did have a lot of fun—a lot of hard work—don't get me wrong. Practice from eight to ten hours a day. It was brutal! But you know what? It was all worth it."

A MIND AND BODY WORKOUT

Ballroom dancing is not just a workout for the body, but for the mind as well. Actors and actresses who can memorize pages of dialogue often could not believe how hard it was to remember the steps to each ballroom dance. Learning the dance steps is especially difficult for celebrities who have primary jobs in places other than Hollywood. When *All My Children* actress Susan Lucci appeared on *DWTS* during Season 7, she continued to work on the famed soap opera, which is filmed in New York. But Lucci said that if she had it to do all over again she would probably take a leave of absence from *All My Children* to appear on *Dancing with the Stars*. She said in an interview with *TV Guide:* "I think to learn these dances in four days is challenging enough. But working on both coasts, we only had the evenings to practice. I don't mean to whine at all—I'm so thrilled with everything that happened—but to do this justice, I think you should simply focus on this, which is plenty."

Professional athletes like Emmitt Smith have spoken about the physical challenges of dancing on the show. Emmitt, pictured with his partner Cheryl Burke, was the winner of *DWTS*'s third season.

4

A Really Big Show

Putting on any live television program is a difficult task, but staging a live show like *Dancing with the Stars* can be overwhelming. So many elements of the show have to fall in place for the production to come off flawlessly. One of them is camerawork.

Even professional dancers are not used to working on a ballroom dance floor that has no less than 10 cameras following them around during a live dance performance. It is even more difficult for celebrity dancers to get comfortable performing before a small army of cameramen and lighting crew members. Undoubtedly, that awkwardness adds to the preshow jitters.

On show days, rehearsals start early in the morning and take place with the cameras. This way, camera operators can see the dances and **choreograph** their own moves. The camera operators often have to make as many fancy moves as the dancers. Planning ahead helps them know when to go in for a close-up or pull back to clearly show kicks and turns, and where to be to get a good angle to capture a breathtaking spin. The camerawork is done to give the TV audience a crisp and sharp view of all the dancers' moves.

WORKING BEHIND THE SCENES

There is always plenty of action on *Dancing with the Stars*, and much of it is hidden from the viewers. That action is taking place in the director's gallery, where a team of behind-the-scenes specialists are literally making hundreds of split-second decisions on exactly what is going over the airwaves, from views of the audience to shots of the band and interviews with the celebrities after their dance numbers. Lighting is also part of the mix, and decisions about how to light up the stage are also made during the technical rehearsal on the day of the show.

While the celebrities only have about four days to learn each new dance, costume designers, makeup artists, and hairstylists are working under the same tight deadline

Many camera operators are needed to make sure that television audiences get the best view of the dancers in action.

to come up with just the right look for each dancer. The dancers have to look utterly glamorous. They have to *exude* excitement. That is all part of the *aura* of the show. Each dancer's costume is designed from scratch, so contestants have to go through several fittings

Fast Fact

Those fancy dresses on *Dancing with the Stars* do not come cheap. Some of the dresses cost upwards of $7,000 each. They are handmade and must be perfectly fitted in just several days.

before the live performance show every Monday. This is in addition to spending eight or nine hours a day practicing their dance routines.

As the competition enters its final weeks, the dancing duos usually perform two live dances a week. That means double duty for the behind-the-scenes team of costume designers, makeup artists, and hair-stylists. When there are costume changes during the live shows, hair and makeup usually have to be redone as well—all in a matter of minutes.

Celebrities who are not eliminated from the competition on the Tuesday results show will find out right after that show what dance they will be performing live the following Monday during the next round of *DWTS*. Once that is revealed, the band swings into action.

Fast Fact

No wardrobe malfunctions allowed! A fellow has to be able to move on the dance floor, but on live TV there is not much room for error, so every pair of pants the male dancers wear is reinforced three times.

MUSIC: A KEY ELEMENT

The music is a major part of the show, and planning for the musical offerings starts months before the show even airs. When the network schedules each season of *Dancing with the Stars,* show producers provide the show's music editor with a list of songs they feel would work well on the show that season. The music editor then matches each song with a ballroom dance. It is important to match classic dances with contemporary songs to give the show that up-to-the-minute, cutting-edge feel.

Celebrities can choose the song they would like to dance to from the list of songs the producers put together that season. However, sometimes more than one celebrity chooses the same song. When that happens, one star is diplomatically asked to choose another song.

Each dance lasts for a minute and 30 seconds. Once celebrities know what dance they are going to do, music director Harold Wheeler, his 17-member band, and four singers start rehearsing the songs for the upcoming show. The band includes some of Los Angeles' top studio musicians. All are familiar with the "We need it fast and we need it good" pace of the show.

One of the executive producers on the show, Conrad Green, believes the fresh musical arrangements and the live band and singers all give the show an exciting feel. "There is a certain dead-ness if you play a commercial track that's exactly what you've heard before," he explained to *Variety* magazine. "Real music, that live element, is an enormous part of why the show works."

Wheeler also plays the show's theme live as the program goes into and comes out of commercial breaks. *Cues* to start the music come to Wheeler from the director's gallery. He has to follow them exactly, or the show looks sloppy.

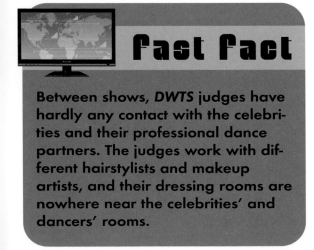

Fast Fact

Between shows, *DWTS* judges have hardly any contact with the celebrities and their professional dance partners. The judges work with different hairstylists and makeup artists, and their dressing rooms are nowhere near the celebrities' and dancers' rooms.

Award-winning African-American composer and conductor Harold Wheeler (left) has been the musical director on *Dancing with the Stars* since the show first aired in 2005.

"Harold Wheeler and our band are unsung heroes, and the singers are fantastic," head judge Len Goodman told *Variety*. "Whatever is thrown at them, they can do. Lindy hop, hip-hop, swing, every genre of music, they cope brilliantly."

THE RIGHT CELEBRITY TEMPERAMENT

Then there are the celebrities, who have to have the right temperament to be in the hustle-bustle atmosphere of a live show every week and have a go-with-the-flow attitude. Deena Katz, *DWTS* senior talent producer, no longer has difficulty getting stars to appear on the show, as she once did when the untested show first went on the air in 2005. Katz told TheWrap.com, "I get hundreds of submissions of people who want to be on. But even if someone who comes to me isn't right for the show, it might spark me to think of someone else in their arena."

She went on to say that booking celebrities for the show is much easier now because many stars are familiar with *DWTS* and know what

Stars Dancing with Stars?

As *DWTS* continued to grow in popularity, its team of professional dancers started to become well known. These dancers started making appearances and going on talk shows like *Larry King Live* and *The Oprah Winfrey Show*. Fans of *Dancing with the Stars* started to recognize their favorites—Cheryl Burke, Tony Dovolani, Edyta Sliwinska, and Alec Mazo, as a few examples. One of the professional dancers, Julianne Hough, even launched a country-western singing career while on the show. Her brother, Derek, also a professional dancer on the show, and Mark Ballas, another *DWTS* regular dancer, formed a band called the Ballas Hough Band (BHB).

DWTS professional hoofers Maksim Chmerkovskiy and Kym Johnson have appeared in the Broadway dance spectacular *Burn the Floor*, while other dancing pros from the show have traveled with *Dancing with the Stars—The Tour*, a road version of the popular reality show that is staged in arenas all over the United States. Many of the pro dancers have built an adoring fan base by displaying their dedicated teaching skills and turning some hapless celebrities into sure-footed, confident dancers.

The professional dancers are an important element of the show. During Season 9 the female dancers included (front, l-r) Karina Smirnoff, Anna Demidova, Lacey Schwimmer, Cheryl Burke, Chelsie Hightower, (back) Edyta Sliwinska, Kym Johnson, and Anna Trebunskaya.

DWTS Season 5 contestant Josie Maran (seated, back) and professional dancer Karina Smirnoff (front) have their hair and makeup done before the show.

appearing on the show can do for their careers. Katz feels pressure when booking celebrities on the popular show now, because "the audience is expecting more. Not only do I have to get bigger names, I have to keep doing something different. We can't have the audience thinking the cast is boring."

TWO CASTS: CELEBS AND PROFESSIONALS

What sets *Dancing with the Stars* apart from other reality shows is that it actually has two casts. Along with the stars, who are brought in to learn the dizzying array of dances for the competition, there are the professional dancers who teach the celebrities the tricks of the trade. Part of what makes *Dancing with the Stars* work and keeps the audience tuning in week after week is how likable the professional dancers are and how well they work with the celebrities. In fact, many of the dancers have developed their own fan followings.

Pairing stars with professional dancers is not done randomly. Senior talent producer Katz said looks, age, personality, and height are just a few of the considerations that go into making the pairings come out just right. The chemistry between the partners is very important because that is what makes the audience care about the dance teams and want to follow the show. "The main thing is to make sure that [partners] get along," Katz told the *New York Daily News.* "You're taking two people that don't know each other and are throwing them together in a situation that's very intense."

To make the show come out right, the professional dancers have to be exceptionally good teachers. They have to be able to break each

Former Olympic skater Kristi Yamaguchi practices with her professional partner, Mark Ballas, during Season 6, which aired in 2008. The hard work between shows paid off, as Kristi and Mark became the first dancers to receive a perfect score of 90—meaning they received perfect 10s from all three judges for three dances during one round of competition. Kristi would go on to win the Mirrorball Trophy in Season 6.

dance down and teach it to their celebrity partner. They also have to come up with a choreography that fits both the music and the celebrity's personality. The dances performed by the competing couples are designed to showcase the celebrities, not the professional dancers. The professional dancers naturally can show off their talent, yet they have to be **understated**. On a live show, the dance goes on no matter what, so even if a celebrity misses a step or slips, they keep going. The professional dancers, some of whom have been world champions, have to learn to live without perfection. No matter what, it is up to the professional dancers to keep their celebrity partners focused, determined, confident, and relaxed when it is time to go out and dance.

To make the viewers feel as though they are truly involved in every aspect of the celebrities' journey on *DWTS*, cameras film each celebrity's practice sessions and record the laughter, tears, frustration, and tension involved in learning the complicated steps to these ballroom dances. **Snippets** of these recorded practice sessions are dropped in throughout the live show. They let viewers see that these couples are really serious about what they are doing. Viewers hear the actual give-and-take between the celebrities and their professional dancer partners as the stars learn new dance steps in a few pressure-packed days. With two weekly live shows involving so many people, plus practice sessions in between, *Dancing with the Stars* might just have the hardest-working cast and crew on television.

5

Sabrina Bryan dances with Mark Ballas during the fifth season of *Dancing with the Stars*. Her surprise elimination is considered one of the show's most shocking moments.

Totally Unpredictable

What is the best thing anyone can say about a reality TV show? That it is totally unpredictable. The more unpredictable the show, the bigger the audience. Reality show fans have proven that they love surprises. Through the years, *Dancing with the Stars* has not failed to showcase its share of the unexpected.

A MAJOR UPSET

One of *Dancing with the Stars'* biggest shockers came during Season 5, on October 30, 2007, when singer Sabrina Bryan (of Disney's Cheetah Girls group) and her professional dance partner, Mark Ballas, were eliminated from the competition in the sixth week. Many people thought the couple would win the competition that season. Bryan and Ballas had earned consistently high scores from the judges throughout the early weeks of the show. In the fourth week, the judges awarded the dancing duo a perfect 30 score for their *paso doble*, making them the first couple to earn a perfect score so early in the competition. The pair had the

highest scores from the judges in weeks 1, 3, and 4. The elimination in week 6 was so unexpected that other celebrities on the show, members of the studio audience, and even some of the judges themselves started to cry when the news was announced.

Bryan has been invited back to dance on *DWTS* several times and has always put on a rousing performance. However, the shock of her elimination still *resonates* with fans, who often bring it up when certain couples are mentioned as shoo-ins for the finals. In a poll conducted by America Online (AOL), the Bryan-Ballas elimination was voted as the Most Shocking TV Event of 2007.

Sabrina Bryan never harbored any ill will toward the show, just gratitude for all the support she received afterwards. As she told *TV Guide*:

"For the producers and the talent to come up to us after the show was amazing, because they were so upset. [Judge] Carrie Ann [Inaba] was in tears. And when I saw her at The View a few days later, she was still emotional about it."

A FAINTING SPELL . . .

Season 5 contained other drama as well. On October 22, 2007, entertainer Marie Osmond fainted during the judges' *critique* of her samba with professional dance partner Jonathan Roberts. Osmond collapsed to the floor as one of the judges was speaking. For a few awkward seconds, no one knew for sure exactly what was wrong with the singer.

Entertainer Marie Osmond dances with partner Jonathan Roberts during the show's fifth season in 2007. Although Marie faced several problems during the season, she still managed to reach the finals. She finished third overall.

As *DWTS* staff ran to her aid, the live show cut away for a commercial. After the show returned from the commercial break, host Tom Bergeron told the audience that Osmond had simply fainted. She was fine, and returned at the end of the evening's broadcast. Later, Osmond discussed the incident, saying, "once in a while, that happens to me when I get winded."

...THEN DEATH IN THE FAMILY

Several weeks later, on the morning of the results show for Week 7, Marie Osmond's father, George, died at age 90. She did not appear on that show and there was some doubt about whether she would return to the competition at all. But she was back for Week 8 and dedicated her performances to the memory of her father.

Earlier in the season, actress Jane Seymour's mother, Mieke, died on the night of the performance show on October 1, 2007. Seymour performed her dance and then left to be with her family. She missed the results show the next night, but also returned to the competition.

INJURIES ON THE DANCE FLOOR

On April 28, 2008 during the seventh week of Season 6, actor Cristian de la Fuente and his professional dance partner, Cheryl Burke, heard a crack as they danced the samba. De la Fuente winced in pain and could not complete the dance. The judges scored the couple on the uncompleted dance and the actor was rushed to the hospital. The next night it was revealed on the results show that de la Fuente had **ruptured** the tendon in his left bicep (the upper arm) and needed an operation to repair the damage. The tough actor from Chile opted to continue in the competition before undergoing the surgery. Because of the injury de la Fuente could not do any lifts, yet he and Burke still managed to finish third in the competition.

During the second week of competition on Season 8, *DWTS* fans were surprised to hear that daredevil Steve-O was unable to perform live on the March 16, 2009, show after falling that day in rehearsals and hurting his back. Steve-O had a reputation for pulling off much more daring stunts than ballroom dancing, but when the former *Wildboyz* star fell while rehearsing the salsa, he landed on his mobile microphone pack and he was in too much pain to continue. The judges based their scores on a dress rehearsal tape of Steve-O and his dance partner, Lacey Schwimmer, and those scores, along with the viewers' votes, were good enough to keep the couple on the show. Steve-O and Schwimmer were eventually eliminated in Week 6.

At least Steve-O got a chance to compete. Rodeo star Ty Murray and his wife, pop singer Jewel Kilcher, were supposed to go head-to-head in competition on *Dancing with the Stars* in Season 8, but never got the chance. Before the season began, Jewel fractured both of her tibias (shinbones) during preshow practice sessions. She had to be replaced on the show by model Holly Madison. Although Jewel came to every show to watch her husband compete and also sang on the show during Season 8, she never danced in what would have been the first time a celebrity husband and wife competed against each other on *Dancing with the Stars*.

Some Controversy, too!

Next to being unpredictable, the best thing a reality show has going for it is controversy. Disputes get people talking about the show, and then others tune in to see what everybody is talking about. Few could argue when Olympic ice skater Kristi Yamaguchi (Season 6) and model Brooke Burke (Season 7) claimed their championships. But other winners have sparked debate among fans.

In Season 2, fans believed that actor Mario Lopez and his professional dance partner, Karina Smirnoff, should have won the Mirrorball Trophy. Instead, the prize went to former NFL star Emmitt Smith and his partner, Cheryl Burke. When Olympic gymnast Shawn Johnson and professional dancer Mark Ballas narrowly defeated actor Gilles Marini and his partner, Cheryl Burke, many fans thought Marini had been the better dancer throughout the competition. But even the judges felt Johnson had put on a better performance during the finals to snare the title. When entertainer Donny Osmond thrilled fans by taking the crown in Season 9, some diehard *DWTS* fans felt singer Mya was better.

Remember: A champion is chosen based on what happens during the finals, the last week of the competition, not a cumulative score over the course of the entire show. Of course, a contestant has to be good enough to make it to the finals.

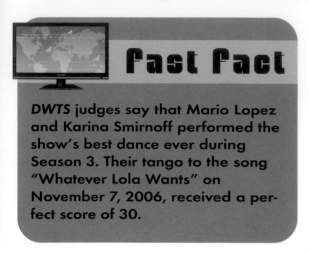

Just two days before Season 8 was to get underway, another injury sidelined contestant Nancy O'Dell, the co-host of *Access Hollywood* at the time. She suffered a torn meniscus, a knee injury that required surgery to repair. *DWTS* producers had to scurry around to find a last-minute replacement for her. They came up with former Dallas Cowboys cheerleader Melissa Rycroft, who had appeared on the 13th season of *The Bachelor*.

Fans of *DWTS* didn't know what to expect from Rycroft. She had less than 48 hours to learn her first dance for the show. Despite the suspense, Rycroft delivered. She became a true contender on the show, eventually finishing third. As *DWTS* senior talent producer Katz told TheWrap.com:

> **"She was my Cinderella story. I called her and said, 'You have two days to learn the dance.' She took a leap of faith, and it was just perfect timing."**

But even Rycroft could not avoid the injury jinx of Season 8. She fractured her ribs during the eighth week of the competition. For a short time, it was not known whether she could continue. But Rycroft *soldiered on*, becoming one of the many celebrities who fought through injuries sustained in the competition to stay in the show.

DREAMS DASHED

When Olympic volleyball star Misty May-Treanor hurt her leg during a training session just before Season 7's third week, she wanted to go on, but she could not put any weight on her leg. It turned out that the pop she heard while practicing the lindy hop was her left Achilles tendon rupturing. It required emergency surgery. Her withdrawal from *DWTS* just before the October 6, 2008, show took viewers

Fast Fact

The lowest score ever recorded on *Dancing with the Stars* came in Season 2, when rapper Master P got an 8 out of a possible 30 for his *paso doble*.

by surprise, especially because the two-time Olympic gold medal winner was one of the favorites to win the competition.

One of the most unexpected aspects of *DWTS* is the number of celebrity injuries connected with the show. Part of the blame has been placed on the **rigors** of the eight- to nine-hour daily practice sessions. The show has now adopted a rule limiting practices to five hours a day to try to cut down on injuries. But as *Dancing with the Stars* judge Carrie Ann Inaba points out, it is the commitment of the stars themselves to do well on the show that has led them to work so hard and put in such long hours. That commitment is what makes *Dancing with the Stars* such a popular program, and will likely keep it among the most-watched reality shows on television for years to come.

Chronology

2004: *Strictly Come Dancing* debuts on May 15 in England.

2005: *Dancing with the Stars* debuts on June 1 on ABC-TV to an audience of 13.5 million; first results show held on September 22 to announce the winner of the Kelly Monaco-John O'Hurley dance-off.

2006: Season 2 of *Dancing with the Stars* premiers on January 5; the show wins its first Emmys on August 27, one for Outstanding Technical Direction, camerawork, video for a series and one for Outstanding Costumes for a Variety or Music Program; *Dancing with the Stars—The Tour* kicks off its first live touring show on September 19, in San Diego, with stars from the show. The tour reaches 38 cities.

2007: *Dancing with the Stars* releases its first DVD spinoff, called *Dancing with the Stars: Cardio Dance*, on April 3; Actress and singer Sabrina Bryan, who consistently put up high scores for her dancing routines on *DWTS*, is eliminated from the competition on October 30. The elimination is voted "most shocking TV event of 2007" in an AOL poll.

2008: The 100th episode of *Dancing with the Stars* airs on May 6; 82-year-old Cloris Leachman takes to the dance floor on September 22, becoming the oldest *DWTS* competitor ever on *Dancing with the Stars.*

2009: Olympic gold medal–winning gymnast Shawn Johnson narrowly defeats actor Gilles Marini on May 19 to win the Season 8 competition. It is the smallest margin of victory in the history of *DWTS*; the show opens Season 9 with its first three-night premiere, on September 21–23.

2010: Season 7 champ Brooke Burke is named the show's new cohost before Season 10 begins; on May 25, Nicole Scherzinger is crowned the winner of Season 10.

Glossary

aura—overall impression.

backbiting—bad-mouthing; spreading nasty and false rumors.

choreograph—to create a dance routine.

critique—review of a performance.

cues—signals to performers to begin a specific action, such as playing music or dancing.

defused—made less tense.

eked out—narrowly succeeded.

exude—give off; radiate.

grueling—very difficult.

hoofers—a slang term for dancers.

incalculable—unable to be calculated or quantified.

relentless—persistent.

resonates—echoes.

rigors—stress and strain; pressures.

ruptured—broken or torn, as a tendon or bone.

sashaying—walking or gliding on the floor in a way that calls attention to oneself.

snippets—small pieces of something, such as film.

soldiered on—continued doing something difficult, despite hardship.

understated—modest and unassuming.

vie—compete.

Resources

FURTHER READING

Baker, Kel, & Ralf Schiller. *Strictly Come Dancing: Step by Step Dance Class: Dance Yourself Fit with the Beginner's Guide to All the Dances from the Show.* London: BBC Books, 2009.

Fox Reality Channel Staff. *The Encyclopedia of Reality Television: The Ultimate Guide to Over 20 Years of Reality TV from the Real World to Dancing with the Stars.* New York: Simon & Schuster, 2008.

Goodman, Len. *Better Late Than Never: My Story.* London: Edury Press, 2008.

Maloney, Alison. *Strictly Come Dancing: The Official 2010 Annual.* London: BBC Books, 2009.

Ovellette, Laurie. *Reality TV: Reality Television Culture*, 2nd ed. New York: NYU Press, 2008.

INTERNET RESOURCES

www.abc.go.com/shows/dancing-with-the-stars

The official ABC-TV network Web site of *Dancing with the Stars.*

www.bbc.co.uk/strictlycomdancing/

The official Web site of *Strictly Come Dancing*, the British version of *Dancing with the Stars.*

www.puredwts.com

A site for fans of *Dancing with the Stars.* Includes history as well as breaking news about the show.

www.buddytv.com/dancing-with-the-stars.aspx

An unofficial site for *Dancing with the Stars* with photos, videos, trivia, and behind-the-scenes news.

Numbers in **bold italics** refer to captions.

ROBERT GRAYSON is an award-winning former daily newspaper reporter and magazine writer. He is the author of a number of books for young adults, including biographies on actors and professional sports figures. His published work has appeared in magazines such as the *New York Yankees Magazine, NBA Hoop, Films of the Golden Age,* and *Big Reel.* Robert has also written books on historical events, animals in show business, and careers for young people. He has watched *Dancing with the Stars* since it debuted in 2005.